Mindfulness for Busy Professionals

Practical Mindfulness Techniques for Stressed Professionals to Improve Focus and Productivity

Dr. Miles J. Cooper

DISCLAIMER

This book is intended for informational and educational purposes only. While Mindfulness for Busy Professionals provides practical mindfulness techniques designed to reduce stress, improve focus, and enhance productivity, it should not be used as a substitute for professional medical or mental health advice. The content is based on current research, general principles of mindfulness, and the author's experience, but individual results may vary. Always consult a qualified health mindfulness professional for personalized advice related to mental health or medical concerns. The author and publisher are not liable for any outcomes resulting from the application of the information provided in this book.

Table of content

Introduction

In the present quick moving world, professionals are exploring expanding requests and extraordinary tensions in their vocations. As assumptions rise, many find themselves continually "on," shuffling endless undertakings while wrestling with stress and exhaustion. The very devices and innovation intended to assist us with working all the more effectively frequently appear to just add to our responsibility, leaving us feeling overpowered, diverted, and, on occasion, drained.

For professionals who feel caught in this cycle, Mindfulness for Occupied Professionals offers a commonsense solution. This book isn't tied in with adding one more thing to your generally full daily agenda; rather, it presents little, basic mindfulness practices that fit flawlessly into even the most active schedule. In doing as such, mindfulness becomes a remedy to stress as well as a device for clearness, flexibility, and improved efficiency.

In this presentation, we will investigate the reason and vision of the book, providing you with a set of how mindfulness can help your work and prosperity. You'll perceive the way little, feasible practices can assist you with recovering your concentration, balance your stress, and carry a more noteworthy feeling of direction to both your professional and individual life.

Why Mindfulness Matters for Professionals

Mindfulness might seem like a far off idea, one related with calm retreats or meditation pads in serene settings. In any case, mindfulness isn't restricted to these spots; it is a useful way to deal with bringing full, non-critical mindfulness into the current second — any place you are, including the work environment. By establishing your consideration in the present, mindfulness permits you to address the day to day requests of professional existence without becoming overpowered by them.

The worth of mindfulness lies in its flexibility. It requires no unique gear or additional time cut out of a generally bustling day. All things being equal, mindfulness meets you right where you are, whether you're stranded in rush hour gridlock, dealing with a troublesome discussion, or dealing with a high-stakes project. Practicing mindfulness implies completely captivating with what you're doing progressively, assisting you with decreasing stress, improve concentration, and pursue choices with a quiet, clear brain.

Various professionals who have integrated mindfulness into their schedules report extraordinary outcomes. One leader, for example, found that requiring only a couple of moments every morning to focus himself with mindfulness breathing permitted him to move toward his day with expanded persistence and concentration. Rather than feeling fatigued by consecutive gatherings, he turned out to be more present, finding that he really finished less distractions. This story represents what many investigations have shown: mindfulness empowers individuals to move toward difficulties with a reasonable psyche and upgraded efficiency.

The Developing Importance of Mindfulness in The Present Work environment

As working environments develop, so too do the assumptions put on professionals. Current workplaces underline efficiency, responsiveness, and versatility. However, for every one of the progressions in productivity, studies uncover a disturbing pattern: rising degrees of stress, burnout, and mental exhaustion among laborers. The quick moving climate that guarantees proficiency frequently leaves individuals feeling depleted, forfeiting their psychological prosperity for the sake of efficiency. Here, mindfulness arises not as a liberal extravagance but rather as a basic professional for supporting long-haul efficiency and emotional well-being.

Organizations are starting to perceive the advantages of supporting mindfulness practices. Numerous associations, from tech goliaths to medical mindfulness suppliers, have coordinated mindfulness programs into their health drives. For instance, Google offers its representatives courses in mindfulness, empowering them to enjoy mindfulness reprieves and take on practices that can upgrade their balance between fun and serious activities. These drives signal a change in how professionals can adjust to an undeniably demanding working environment without undermining their emotional wellness. Mindfulness, it ends up, isn't simply an individual excursion but a vital aspect for establishing more practical and adjusted workplaces.

This book offers a tool compartment for individual professionals to coordinate mindfulness into their work schedules. From procedures like mindfulness breathing and meditation to techniques for developing mindfulness communication and the capacity to understand anyone on a deeper level, you'll learn exercises that don't expect you to change your set of working responsibilities or everyday requests. These instruments assist you in approaching your obligations with a stronger outlook, transforming everyday undertakings into valuable open doors for development and fulfillment.

How This Book Can Assist You with Flourishing?

Mindfulness for Occupied Professionals is planned with the real factors of a cutting-edge profession as a top priority. The parts of this book give an organized, open manual for understanding and practicing mindfulness in manners that line up with the requests of an professional way of life. This isn't a manual for getting away from work stress by withdrawing from your obligations; rather, it's tied in with furnishing you with devices to change how you draw in with those obligations.

Every section is loaded with pragmatic strategies that can be applied progressively in settings. For instance, you'll track down techniques for managing testing discussions with colleagues, overseeing upsetting activities, and in any event, settling on additional mindfulness choices. Every strategy is made to take a couple of seconds, guaranteeing it's reasonable regardless of how occupied your day might be.

The book is separated into clear areas that form dynamically on one another. To start with, you'll acquire a comprehension of what mindfulness is, including a glance at its underlying foundations, its logical premise, and its particular advantages for professionals. Then, you'll be acquainted with useful procedures for applying mindfulness in day to day existence, from basic breathing activities to mindfulness communication techniques. At long last, we'll cover how to carry out mindfulness reliably in your work life, offering direction for beating obstructions and keeping a feasible practice.

Toward the finish of this excursion, you'll know how to practice mindfulness as well as how to make it an amazing asset for accomplishing more prominent concentration, decreasing stress, and expanding position fulfillment. This book is tied in with assisting you with becoming a more powerful professional as well as a more satisfied one.

A Functional Way to deal with Enduring Change

Executing a mindfulness practice doesn't mean redesigning your life or your day-to-day plan. All things considered, it's about little changes in the way you think, act and answer. By rolling out these little improvements, you step by step train your cerebrum to turn out to be more versatile, strong, and centered. This is the force of brain adaptability, an idea we'll dig into later in the book, which demonstrates the way that your mind can change and adjust to better approaches to thinking and answering.

We should take, for example, a typical situation for professionals: performing multiple tasks. In our rapid work culture, performing various tasks frequently feels like a need, yet concentrating on showing it fundamentally lessens efficiency and increments stress. Through mindfulness, you'll figure out how to move toward tasks with a determined center that further develops efficiency as well as decreases the feeling of overpower. You'll find ways of focusing on undertaking mindfulness, tackling distractions, and remaining focused — even in a speedy climate.

The focal point of this book is on functional, reasonable applications. You won't find complex hypotheses or extensive practices that require a total way of life redesign. All things being equal, you'll find instruments that work inside the design of your ongoing daily practice, making mindfulness open, significant, and reasonable.

A Dream for Individual and Professional Development

As you leave on this excursion, realize that mindfulness isn't simply a technique for overcoming the business day; it's a strong method for improving your general personal satisfaction. The methods in this book act as pathways to fabricate flexibility, sustain mindfulness, and develop an outlook that flourishes despite difficulties. Thus, mindfulness can emphatically affect your work as well as your relationships, psychological wellness, and prosperity.

Professionals frequently invest such a lot of energy zeroing in on making outer progress that they neglect their inner requirements. This book welcomes you to move that equilibrium. Envision beginning every day with a reasonable psyche, serenely exploring through difficulties, and finishing the day with a feeling of fulfillment and reason. That is the vision of mindfulness for occupied professionals — a dream of a decent, successful, and satisfying work life.

As we push ahead, recall that mindfulness is an excursion, one that becomes further with training and persistence. This book is here to direct you end route, offering functional help and bits of knowledge that will make each step available and fulfilling. Whether you're new to mindfulness or hoping to develop your training, Mindfulness for Occupied Professionals means to outfit you with all that you want to transform this vision into a reality.

Part 1: Understanding Mindfulness

Chapter 1: The Benefits of Mindfulness for Busy Professionals

In this day and age of steady requests and moment reactions, numerous professionals feel trapped in a ceaseless pattern of undertakings, cutoff times, and assumptions. The strain to accomplish more, answer quicker, and produce improved results frequently prompts a condition of persistent stress and mental fatigue. Yet, imagine a scenario in which there was a method for moving toward work that assists you with fulfilling needs as well as further develops your prosperity and efficiency. This is the commitment to mindfulness — training that has been demonstrated to assist innumerable people with overseeing stress, upgrading the center, and carrying a feeling of quiet to even the most active days.

In this part, we'll investigate what mindfulness implies, how it benefits professionals, and why it's remarkably fit to help those shuffling high-stress professions. As you'll see, mindfulness offers undeniably more than a passing snapshot of quiet; it gives a structure to moving toward existence with clearness, versatility, and reason.

Meaning of Mindfulness

At its center, mindfulness is the act of carrying your active focus to the current second, with a demeanor of receptiveness and non-judgment. As opposed to allowing your brain to meander into remorseful thoughts or future tensions, mindfulness secures you in the present time and place, permitting you to completely draw in with anything that task or experience is before you.

For professionals, this present-centered approach can be extraordinary. Rather than performing multiple tasks or responding incautiously to new difficulties, mindfulness urges you to move toward each task with a quiet, purposeful mentality. This shift can prompt more clear reasoning, more compelling navigation, and a more prominent feeling of fulfillment in your work. Training reminds you to stop, notice, and answer nicely, instead of just responding to the many requests around you.

Mindfulness isn't just about calming the brain; it's tied in with developing mindfulness and goals in each part of your day. This mindfulness can reach out to seeing what stress means for you, figuring out your responses to challenges, and perceiving designs that might be obstructing your adequacy. As you become more mindful, you construct the psychological clearness and versatility expected to explore both the normal and unprecedented tensions of professional life.

Significance of Mindfulness in the Working Environment

The working environment today is more mind-boggling and demanding than at any other time in recent memory. Professionals are frequently expected to shuffle different jobs, remain associated external normal hours, and consistently adjust to changing advances and assumptions. This climate, however wealthy in an open door, can prompt uplifted stress and burnout.

Mindfulness offers a method for offsetting requests. By developing mindfulness, professionals can upgrade their capacity to oversee stress, remain on track, and answer smoothly to difficulties. Rather than feeling constrained by their plans for the day or overpowered by their obligations, mindful professionals figure out how to move toward each undertaking with a grounded viewpoint.

Work environments that help mindfulness drives additionally see unmistakable advantages. Groups that train mindfulness report expanded joint effort, decreased struggle, and surer work culture. This is because mindfulness assists people with dealing with their stress as well as advances more prominent compassion and persistence in collaborations with partners. At the point when professionals approach their work and their associations with mindfulness, they add to a climate where everybody can flourish.

A developing collection of exploration upholds these perceptions. Studies have shown that professionals who practice mindfulness exhibit more noteworthy work fulfillment, decreased stress, and upgraded center. By cultivating mindfulness, working environments are putting resources into their most prominent resource — the prosperity and efficiency of their kin.

Advantages of Mindfulness for Focused on Professionals

Mindfulness gives a scope of advantages that are especially significant for occupied professionals. We should investigate the absolute most significant benefits:

1. Upgraded Concentration and Focus

One of the essential advantages of mindfulness is its capacity to further develop the center. Numerous professionals battle with distractions, whether from outside sources like email notices or inner sources like concern and stress. Mindfulness prepares the brain to remain secured to a solitary undertaking, diminishing the inclination to hop among exercises and upgrading generally speaking focus.

Envision a professional entrusted with setting up a mind-boggling report while at the same time handling messages and calls. Without mindfulness, the brain might feel dispersed, hopping between undertakings without finishing any of them. With mindfulness, nonetheless, you can foster the professionalize to zero in eagerly on the report, then, at that point, concentrate entirely on different tasks each in turn. This engaged methodology further develops effectiveness as well as prompts better work.

2. Stress Decrease

In a high-stress calling, many individuals work in a steady "survival" mode. This state might be powerful in snapshots of genuine emergencies, however after some time, persistent stress can wear out both mental and actual wellbeing. Mindfulness intrudes on this cycle by assisting people with overseeing stress proactively. By establishing yourself right now, mindfulness decreases the propensity to catastrophize or become consumed by stresses over what's in store.

Practices like mindful breathing and meditation trigger the body's unwinding reaction, balancing the impacts of stress chemicals and advancing a feeling of quiet. For instance, taking a couple of full breaths during a strained gathering can help you re-focus, diminishing tension and empowering you to answer with levelheadedness instead of reactivity.

3. Further developed Independent direction

The high speed of the cutting-edge working environment frequently requires fast choices. In any case, going with choices under stress can cloud judgment, prompting decisions dependent more upon criticalness than mindfulness. Mindfulness assists you with slowing down, surveying circumstances with more noteworthy clearness, and settling on choices from a position of quiet instead of strain.

At the point when you practice mindfulness, you foster a capacity to notice your considerations without becoming overpowered by them. This mindfulness assists you with perceiving inclinations or routine reactions that might be affecting your independent direction. Thus, you're bound to pick activities that line up with your drawn-out goals and values, in any event, when under tension.

4. Upgraded Ability to understand anyone on a emotional level

Mindfulness advances the capacity to appreciate people on a emotional level by cultivating mindfulness and compassion. Mindfulness empowers you to perceive your emotional triggers and examples, while sympathy helps you comprehend and answer the emotions of others. Together, these characteristics are fundamental for building positive, useful relationships in the working environment.

In circumstances where stress runs intense — like settling a contention or giving criticism — mindfulness can direct you to answer with responsiveness and regard. By practicing mindfulness, you become better prepared to oversee both your emotions and those of your partners, making a more amicable and cooperative workplace.

5. Expanded Versatility and Flexibility

Each professional countenances mishaps, whether it's a missed cutoff time, a troublesome client, or a surprising venture change. Mindfulness fortifies your flexibility by assisting you with exploring these difficulties without becoming deterred. Instead of responding genuinely to mishaps, mindfulness professionals figure out how to stop, survey what is happening impartially, and answer usefully.

This versatility stretches out to overseeing change. In our current reality where enterprises develop quickly, the capacity to adjust is urgent. Mindfulness upholds flexibility by assisting you with staying open to additional opportunities and moving toward change with interest as opposed to fear. It changes obstructions into open doors for development, empowering you to flourish even in questionable circumstances.

Building a Foundation for Mindfulness in Professional Life

Bringing mindfulness into your life as a bustling proficient doesn't demand a significant time speculation or intense way of life changes. The goal is to consolidate mindfulness in manners that are manageable and viable with your everyday daily practice. As this book advances, you'll find various procedures, each fit to various parts of your work and individual life. Whether you're exploring a pressed schedule, driving a group, or overseeing stress, you'll find moves toward that make mindfulness both open and helpful.

Think about beginning with little changes — like saving a couple of moments every day for mindful breathing or taking brief "mindfulness stops" between undertakings. These practices might appear to be straightforward, yet after some time, they can generally move how you experience and answer your professional life.

For example, you could take a stab at practicing mindful relaxing briefly prior to entering a gathering. In doing as such, you're setting yourself up intellectually as well as improving your concentration and lucidity. Or on the other hand, you could take a couple of seconds to practice mindful tuning in during discussions, permitting you to connect all the more completely with partners and clients.

Mindfulness, when reliably practiced, can reclassify your experience of work. There's actually no need to focus on wiping out stress yet about figuring out how to move toward it with quiet and flexibility. By incorporating mindfulness into your professional life, you can move from a condition of steady reactivity to one of smart reaction, making a really satisfying, adjusted, and useful profession.

Chapter 2: What is Mindfulness? A Comprehensive Overview

History and Underlying Foundations of Mindfulness

Mindfulness, however broadly perceived today, follows back millennia, established emotionally in Eastern otherworldly customs, especially Buddhism. In its easiest structure, mindfulness implies zeroing in on one's mindfulness in the current second without judgment. While the idea is frequently connected to strict practices, it means quite a bit to take note that mindfulness, as applied today, rises above any single conviction framework. It has developed to turn into a mainstream practice, exceptionally esteemed for its mental and emotional advantages.

The Western transformation of mindfulness started in the last part of the 1970s when Dr. Jon Kabat-Zinn presented Mindfulness Based Stress Decrease (MBSR), an organized program zeroed in on mitigating persistent torment and stress through mindfulness methods. His work set up a mix of mindfulness in medical services, mental wellbeing, and professional spaces. This shift from emotional roots to an experimentally upheld practice has permitted mindfulness to thrive in a world progressively described by speedy ways of life and stress.

Understanding the historical backdrop of mindfulness assists professionals in valuing its profundity and perceiving that the advantages they look for are based on hundreds of years of training and astuteness. By recognizing it's starting points, occupied professionals can move toward mindfulness with a feeling of regard and interest, investigating ways of fitting the training to their one-of-a-kind requirements.

Key Standards and Ideas

At its center, mindfulness is tied in with developing a non-critical consciousness of the current second. To separate it, mindfulness typifies a few key rules that make it particularly significant and groundbreaking for professionals.

1. Purposeful Mindfulness: Mindfulness urges people to carry deliberate concentration on their activities, considerations, and emotions. Instead of allowing the psyche to meander randomly, this standard advances a cognizant presence, encouraging better independent direction and lessening stress.

2. Non-Critical Perception: A central idea of mindfulness is noticing one's considerations and sentiments without judgment. In a work environment setting, professionals frequently face tensions to rapidly respond. By practicing non-critical perception, one can step back, evaluate circumstances tranquility, and answer mindfully, upgrading relational relationships.

3. Acknowledgment and Persistence: Mindfulness shows acknowledgment of the current second, anything it holds. This doesn't mean surrendering to antagonistic circumstances but instead

recognizing reality. In the professional world, where versatility is critical, this rule can assist people with confronting difficulties with persistence and flexibility, limiting hasty responses.

4. Fledgling's Brain: Moving toward circumstances with a "novice's psyche" includes seeing things as though interestingly, liberated from previously established inclinations. Professionals who embrace this attitude can cultivate inventiveness, critical thinking, and flexibility by reviewing difficulties according to new points of view.

By coordinating these standards, mindfulness empowers professionals to deal with stress all the more successfully, pursue clear choices, and encourage a more grounded way to deal with work and life.

Exposing Normal Mindfulness Myths

Notwithstanding its developing notoriety, numerous confusions about mindfulness continue, making boundaries that might keep professionals from completely embracing the training. We should explain a few normal fantasies.

1. Legend: Mindfulness is Tied in with Discharging the Psyche of Considerations
One of the most common misguided judgments is that mindfulness requires a totally clear brain, liberated from meditations. In actuality, mindfulness isn't tied in with quieting the psyche however about noticing considerations without connection. For a bustling proficient, this implies you don't need to "switch off" your meditations yet essentially remember them. By recognizing meditations without becoming consumed by them, you gain clearness and mental control.

2. Fantasy: Mindfulness is Just for Individuals Who Ponder for quite a long time
Another normal conviction is that mindfulness requires long stretches of meditation, making it difficult to reach for those with occupied plans. Be that as it may, mindfulness can be polished in only a couple of moments daily, and could be coordinated into routine exercises like walking or eating. For a professional, this implies that you can receive the rewards of mindfulness without expecting to commit a lot of time. Little, reliable endeavors can yield critical outcomes.

3. Fantasy: Mindfulness is a Strict Practice
In spite of the fact that mindfulness has establishes in Buddhism, it has developed into a mainstream practice upheld by logical exploration. Mindfulness requires no strict conviction or foundation. For professionals, this implies mindfulness is a commonsense instrument for overseeing stress, upgrading center, and further developing efficiency — open to anybody paying little heed to confidence or emotional connection.

4. Legend: Mindfulness Makes You Inactive or Self-satisfied
Certain individuals dread that mindfulness could make them excessively aloof, lessening their drive to accomplish goals. In truth, mindfulness develops a quiet, engaged mind that can really

build efficiency and lucidity. It doesn't mean tolerating circumstances without activity, but instead answering mindfully. For occupied professionals, this equilibrium can prompt more compelling activity and further developed work results.

Exposing these legends is fundamental for occupied professionals, as it opens up the act of mindfulness to everybody, permitting them to draw in with it everything being equal and without unnecessary strain.

Grasping mindfulness from its verifiable roots, key standards, and present day transformations establishes a strong starting point for integrating it into day to day existence. For occupied professionals, mindfulness is something beyond a pattern — it's a tried and true, deductively upheld way to deal with carrying on with a fair and useful life. By moving past confusions and embracing the genuine substance of mindfulness, professionals can venture out toward a more focused, satisfying vocation.

Chapter 3: The Science Behind Mindfulness

Brain adaptability and Mindfulness

The mind's ability to change and adjust — known as brain adaptability — is quite possibly of the most pivotal revelation in neuroscience. For a really long time, researchers accepted that the cerebrum was basically fixed after a specific age, incapable to develop or develop new brain associations. Nonetheless, research has uncovered that the cerebrum stays versatile over the course of life, continually reshaping itself in light of encounters and ways of behaving. This idea of brain adaptability is fundamental for grasping the logical force of mindfulness.

Mindfulness, as a training, enacts specific regions of the cerebrum liable for center, mindfulness, and emotional guidelines. At the point when an individual consistently participates in mindfulness works, they fortify brain processes that advance a quiet, mindful, and tough perspective. For occupied professionals, this can mean an upgraded capacity to center, work on emotional control during high-stress circumstances, and more noteworthy mental clearness.

Truth be told, studies have demonstrated the way that mindfulness can expand the thickness of the prefrontal cortex, the region of the mind engaged with independent direction, consideration, and character advancement. It additionally emphatically influences the amygdala, the cerebrum's "alert" focus answerable for stress reactions. As professionals explore upsetting conditions, these neurological changes encourage a more adjusted reaction to challenges, taking into consideration smart, estimated responses instead of indiscreet choices driven by stress.

Brain adaptability makes it workable for mindfulness to act as a groundbreaking device in the professional world. After some time, the mindful mind turns out to be better prepared to deal with stresss, tackle issues imaginatively, and deal with emotions effortlessly, straightforwardly adding to more readily work execution and mental prosperity.

Mindfulness and Stress Reduction

In the speedy professional world, stress is often seen as an undeniable result of achievement. In any case, left uncontrolled, constant stress can prompt burnout, diminished efficiency, and, surprisingly, actual medical problems. Mindfulness offers a logically approved way to deal with lessening stress, which is the reason it's undeniably esteemed in work environment settings.

At the point when people practice mindfulness, their bodies take part in an unwinding reaction — a physiological state inverse to the stress reaction. Mindfulness brings down cortisol levels, the chemical connected to stress, assisting people with feeling more quiet and more in charge. This impact isn't simply transitory; normal mindfulness practice can prompt enduring decreases in generally speaking emotions of anxiety, as the mind turns out to be more capable at setting off the unwinding reaction over the stress reaction.

In addition, mindfulness has been displayed to upgrade pulse fluctuation (HRV), which is a sign of how well the body can adjust to stress. Higher HRV is related to flexibility, better close-to-home guidelines, and working on emotional wellness. For occupied professionals, this implies that a reliable mindfulness practice can make a cradle against stress, diminishing its unsafe impacts and assisting them with moving toward every day with an unmistakable, consistent brain.

Mindfulness additionally permits people to turn out to be more mindful of their stress triggers. By distinguishing these triggers, professionals can foster more proactive survival strategies, as opposed to depending on receptive reactions that may not work well for them in the long haul. This mindfulness is significant for breaking the pattern of persistent stress and encouraging a balance between fun and serious activities that support efficiency.

Mindfulness and Efficiency

One of the most convincing explanations behind occupied professionals investigating mindfulness is its effect on efficiency. A long way from being a detached practice, mindfulness effectively develops smartness, concentration, and productivity — all characteristics that add to elite execution in the work environment. Via preparing the psyche to stay present, mindfulness lessens the steady mental "exchanging" that happens when the brain bounces between tasks. Research has shown that this training essentially helps efficiency by decreasing distractions and upgrading fixation.

Mindfulness encourages efficiency through a few components:

1. Improved Concentration: Mindfulness hones consideration by preparing the psyche to zero in on each task in turn. In a world loaded up with distractions, this professionalism is important. Studies uncover that mindfulness preparation can work on supported consideration, permitting professionals to effectively focus on undertakings and complete them more.

2. Decreased Performing various tasks: Performing multiple tasks is much of the time seen as an efficiency supporter, yet it as a rule makes the contrary difference. The human cerebrum isn't intended to deal with various undertakings all the while without a decrease in proficiency and precision. Mindfulness energizes a solitary task center, empowering professionals to finish jobs with more prominent speed and quality, eventually prompting higher efficiency.

3. Further developed Independent direction: Mindfulness upgrades mental adaptability, empowering professionals to settle on better choices under tension. Instead of responding hastily, mindfulness professionals can evaluate circumstances smoothly, think about choices, and pursue thoroughly examined decisions. This can prompt more essential results in both everyday assignments and basic tasks.

4. Increased Emotional Resilience: Emotions, particularly pessimistic ones, can cloud judgment and influence efficiency. Mindfulness encourages emotional versatility, making it more straightforward to explore difficulties without going off track of dissatisfaction, uneasiness, or outrage. By dealing with emotions really, professionals can keep up with energy and concentration, even in tough spots.

5. More prominent Imagination: Innovativeness frequently requires a casual, receptive outlook. At the point when under stress, the mind will in general get into a tight "survival" mode, which smothers imagination. Mindfulness can assist with reducing this inflexibility, advancing a more adaptable, inventive way to deal with critical thinking. This is particularly helpful for jobs that require advancement and out-of-the-container thinking.

In the present high-stress proficient climate, where effectiveness is principal, mindfulness offers a demonstrated way to keep up with as well as improving efficiency. By making mental lucidity and close-to-home equilibrium, mindfulness enables professionals to think about the big picture before attacking the details, bringing about superior results without the expense of burnout.

The science behind mindfulness uncovers a strong, proof-based way to deal with upgrading a proficient life. Brain adaptability shows us that the cerebrum is exceptionally versatile, and with normal mindfulness practice, professionals can reshape their psyches to be more engaged, strong, and quiet. The stress decreasing impacts of mindfulness give a basic cure to the tensions of the cutting edge work environment, while the efficiency advantages of mindfulness permit professionals to accomplish more effortlessly and with less stress.

Part 2: Practical Mindfulness Techniques

Chapter 4: Mindfulness Meditation for Busy Professionals

Getting everything rolling with Mindfulness Meditation

For some professionals, meditation can appear to be an extravagance — a training that requires a lot of time or a total departure from the hecticness of work and life. Be that as it may, mindfulness meditation is interestingly fit to fit inside even the most pressed plans. A long way from demanding broad time responsibilities, mindfulness meditation can be pretty much as brief as a couple of moments daily. When drilled reliably, it significantly affects stress decrease, center, and emotional versatility, making it an important device for occupied professionals.

To begin, think about saving only five to ten minutes in your day. Find a peaceful, agreeable space where you will not be upset. Sit such that feels regular — this may be on a seat, a pad, or in any event, standing assuming that that is more open. The goal is to develop mindfulness and presence, not to accomplish an ideal actual stance. Shut your eyes or relax your look, whichever feels more good, and begin by taking a couple of full breaths to focus yourself.

Start by concentrating on your relaxing. Notice the beat and stream of every breath as it enters and leaves your body. At the point when considerations emerge — and they unavoidably will — recognize them without judgment, and gently return your concentration to the breath. This act of noticing and returning is the groundwork of mindfulness meditation. There's no need to focus on halting considerations yet figuring out how to notice them without becoming mixed up in them. Over the long haul, this basic practice reinforces your capacity to center, lessens stress, and cultivates a quiet, clear psyche.

Assuming you're new to meditation, directed meetings can be unbelievably useful. Numerous applications, for example, Headspace or Quiet, offer brief, organized meetings planned explicitly for occupied people. These directed practices can assist you with fostering a daily schedule and extend how you might interpret mindfulness meditation, permitting you to encounter its advantages regardless of whether you're in a hurry.

Ways to Integrate Meditation into Your Day to day Daily Schedule

Coordinating meditation into a bustling schedule can feel testing, yet with a couple of key changes, it can turn into a characteristic piece of your day-to-day daily schedule. Here are some successful ways of building a supportable meditation practice:

1. Begin Little: Start with a sensible goal, like five minutes every morning. Consistency is a higher priority than span, so focus on a short everyday practice that feels reasonable.

2. Pick a Normal Time: Set a steady time for your meditation practice. Many individuals find that reflecting in the first part of the day establishes an uplifting vibe for the afternoon, while others

favor a night meeting to loosen up. Pick a period that lines up with your normal cadence and plan for getting work done.

3. Connect Meditation to a Current Propensity: One powerful method for building another propensity is to attach it to a current one. For instance, you could reflect just in the wake of cleaning your teeth or not long prior to beginning your working day. Partnering meditation with another everyday schedule supports consistency and makes it simpler to recollect.

4. Utilize Little Breaks Mindfully: On the off chance that you battle to find a devoted block of time, have a go at meshing short meditation minutes into your day. A couple of mindful breaths before a gathering, a short meditation on your mid-day break, or a short delay prior to handling a major undertaking can all add to your general mindfulness practice.

5. Find Responsibility Accomplices: Imparting your goal to a partner or companion can give added motivation. You could try and consider framing a little meditation bunch at work, where you can uphold one another and contemplate together, regardless of whether practical. Knowing you're in good company on this excursion can make it more straightforward to remain steady.

6. Embrace Adaptability: Meditation doesn't need to look similar consistently. Occasionally, you could practice conventional situated meditation; on different days, a mindful walk may be more open. Permitting adaptability guarantees you can keep up with your training even on occupied or eccentric days.

Keep in mind, that meditation isn't about flawlessness. Occasionally will feel more straightforward than others, and that is ordinary. The key is to continue to appear, regardless of whether only for a couple of moments. Over the long haul, these little endeavors compound, making a tough brain and a decent, quiet presence that benefits both individual prosperity and professional execution.

Beating Normal Meditation Impediments

While the advantages of meditation are indisputable, most people experience difficulties while attempting to lay out and keep a meditation practice. Tending to these deterrents proactively can assist you with remaining committed, in any event, when the training feels troublesome.

1. "I Need More Time": This is maybe the most widely recognized hindrance among occupied professionals. To conquer it, begin with only a couple of moments daily. Indeed, even concise snapshots of meditation can yield benefits, particularly whenever practiced reliably. Consider seeing meditation as a psychological "reset" as opposed to a tedious undertaking; this change in outlook can make it more straightforward to focus on.

2. "My Psyche Won't Quit Meandering": It's confusing that meditation requires a still brain. Truly, everybody encounters meandering considerations, particularly from the get-go. Rather than attempting to stop your meditations, essentially notice them and gently divert your concentration to the breath. Over the long haul, your capacity to remain present will get to the next level. Keep in mind, that each time you bring your consideration back, you're preparing your psyche to center, which is the center of mindfulness meditation.

3. "I Don't See Quick Outcomes": Meditation is a training that forms benefits step by step. While certain individuals experience a feeling of quiet immediately, many need half a month or even a long time to see massive changes. To remain roused, help yourself to remember the drawn-out benefits. Considering little wins — like the inclination less receptive during unpleasant circumstances or seeing better concentration — can assist with building up your responsibility.

4. "I Feel Anxious": Actual distress or fretfulness is regular, particularly assuming you're new to standing by for broadened periods. Assuming this occurs, take a stab at changing your situation to one that feels more good. Mindful stretching or emotional breathing before contemplating can likewise assist with decreasing anxiety. You could explore different avenues regarding more limited meetings to construct solace over the long haul.

5. "It's Exhausting": For some purposes, meditation might feel tedious right away. To keep your work on drawing in, take a stab at exploring different avenues regarding various sorts of meditation, such as directed representation or body checks. Every variety offers a new encounter and may resound unexpectedly, assisting with keeping your work fascinating and reasonable.

By expecting and tending to these normal difficulties, you can fabricate a meditation practice that stays consistent even despite hindrances. Keep in mind, that each challenge you defeat fortifies your strength and responsibility, supporting the very characteristics that make meditation so groundbreaking.

Mindfulness meditation is a priceless practice for busy professionals looking to lessen stress, increase center, and develop a decent perspective. By beginning small, integrating meditation into existing schedules, and tending to normal difficulties, you can make training that fits flawlessly into your life, even with requesting plans. Over the long run, these snapshots of mindfulness compound, prompting enduring advantages that decidedly influence both individual and professional domains.

Chapter 5: Mindful Breathing and Movement

Mindful Breathing Activities

In the speedy existences of occupied professionals, breathing frequently becomes shallow and quick, which can expand stress and uneasiness levels without us in any event, acknowledging it. Mindful breathing is a strong yet basic practice that focuses on the current second, grounds the brain, and lessens stress. It tends to be done any place in the middle between gatherings, during a drive, or as a fast reset while feeling overpowered. By taking a couple of seconds to intentionally inhale, you can immediately bring down emotions of anxiety, recapture clearness, and move toward difficulties with a recharged feeling of quiet.

Essential Mindful Breathing Activity

To start, find a tranquil place where you will not be upset for a couple of moments. Begin by sitting in an agreeable position, either in a seat or on the floor, with your spine straight and your hands laying gently on your lap. Shut your eyes or relax your look if that feels good.

Take a sluggish, full breath in through your nose, feeling your chest and mid-region extend. Hold the breath momentarily, then leisurely breathe out through your mouth, seeing how your body unwinds with the delivery. Center around the vibe of the breath as it streams all through your body. Assuming that your psyche begins to meander, tenderly aide your consideration back to your breathing without judgment. Rehash this cycle for a couple of moments, expecting to feel more grounded and focused with every breath.

4-7-8 Breathing Procedure

The 4-7-8 procedure is a well-known and powerful technique for quieting the psyche and body, making it particularly valuable for occupied professionals who experience high emotions of anxiety. This exercise includes breathing in, holding the breath, and afterward breathing out in a controlled succession, which manages the sensory system and encourages unwinding.

1. Breathe discreetly through your nose for a count of four.

2. Pause your breathing for a count of seven.

3. Breathe out totally through your mouth for a count of eight.

Rehash this cycle four to multiple times, zeroing in on each period of the breath. The 4-7-8 example can be utilized whenever you want to unwind rapidly, like before a significant gathering or show.

Box Breathing (Square Relaxing)

Box breathing, or square breathing, is another helpful breathing method that brings mental clearness and dependability. This strategy is frequently drilled by people in high-stress callings, like people on call and military staff, to stay cool-headed under tension.

To practice box relaxing:

1. Breathe in leisurely through your nose to a count of four.

2. Pause your breathing for a count of four.

3. Breathe out leisurely through your mouth to a count of four.

4. Pause your breathing again for a count of four.

Rehash this interaction for a few rounds. As you center around each piece of the breath, your brain becomes retained in the musicality, which can assist with facilitating uneasiness and further developing the center.

These mindful breathing activities are viable devices to oversee stress and assemble versatility. By practicing them reliably, even in short minutes over the day, you'll have the option to make a propensity for quiet, mindful breathing that upholds both mental lucidity and emotional equilibrium.

Mindfulness Development Strategies

Notwithstanding mindfulness breathing, mindfulness development is one more remarkable approach to reconnecting with the body, discharging strain, and working on by and large prosperity. Mindful development includes participating in straightforward, deliberate actual activities that uplift body mindfulness and empower unwinding. By moving the concentration from result-driven actual work to slow, intentional developments, professionals can partake in the advantages of development without the requirement for full exercise.

Gentle Stretching for Stress Alleviation

Gentle stretching can deliver stress that amasses from sitting or remaining similarly situated for expanded periods. Practicing mindfulness permits you to reconnect with your body and notice any areas of snugness or distress. Here is a straightforward stretching activity to attempt at your work area or throughout a break:

1. Neck Stretch: Sit or stand easily. Tenderly slant your head to one side, bringing your ear towards your shoulder, and hold for a couple of breaths. Rehash on the left side. This delivers strain in the neck and shoulders.

2. Shoulder Roll: Roll your shoulders in sluggish circles, first forward, then, at that point, in reverse. Center around the development and notice how it feels in your body. This stretch aids discharge snugness in the upper back and shoulders.

3. Situated Ahead Overlap: Sit with your feet level on the ground and knees bowed. Gradually pivot at your hips, bringing down your chest toward your thighs, and let your arms hang. Inhale emotionally and feel the stretch along your spine and lower back.

Play out these stretches mindfully, focusing on every sensation in your muscles. Moving gradually permits you to tune into areas of stress and completely benefit from each stretch.

Walking Meditation

Walking meditation is an amazing practice for professionals who might feel excessively fretful about situated meditation. It joins development with mindfulness, making it simple to incorporate into day-to-day schedules, for example, walking to a gathering or taking a mid-day break.

To work on walking meditation, begin by finding a peaceful way or space where you can walk undisturbed. Start walking gradually, focusing on each step. Notice the impression of your feet taking off the ground, pushing ahead, and landing once more. Center around the mood of your means and how it feels to move. Assuming your psyche starts to meander, tenderly take it back to the development of your body.

Walking meditation doesn't call for quite a while of responsibility. Indeed, even five minutes of mindful walking can work on mental lucidity, lessen stress, and improve actual mindfulness. This training helps anchor you right now, changing a customary movement into a chance for mindfulness.

Yoga-Propelled Stretches for Professionals

Yoga-motivated extends are likewise a viable method for integrating mindfulness development into a bustling day. These stretches assist with alleviating stress, further develop adaptability, and advance mental unwinding.

1. Mountain Posture (Tadasana): Stand with your feet hip-width separated, and arms at your sides. Take a full breath and lift your arms above, coming towards the roof. Ground your feet and connect with your center, feeling the stretch through your whole body.

2. Situated Contort (Ardha Matsyendrasana): Sit with your spine straight, and get your right leg over your left knee. Put your left hand on your right knee and bend tenderly to the right, involving your right hand on the ground for help. Hold for a couple of breaths, then, at that point, switch sides. This posture extends the spine and delivers strain toward the back.

3. Youngster's Posture (Balasana): Bow on the floor, sit out of sorts, and stretch your arms forward, bringing your brow down to the ground. This posture permits you to unwind, discharge strain, and practice mindful relaxation.

Mindful development doesn't need a rec center or exceptional gear. With a couple of basic strategies, you can integrate gentle, deliberate stretches into your day, upgrading both physical and mental prosperity.

Integrating Mindfulness into Everyday Exercises

Mindfulness can be incorporated into day-to-day exercises past assigned practice times. By pointing out centered routine undertakings, professionals can make every second a mindfulness one, upgrading presence and decreasing stress over the course of the day.

1. Mindful Eating: During dinners or tidbits, take a couple of seconds to see the value in the varieties, surfaces, and smells of your food. Bite gradually, seeing each chomp's flavor and surface. This training assists you with relishing your food, helps with processing, and gives you a break from the surge of the day.

2. Mindful Driving: Rather than hurrying through your drive, attempt to mindfully move toward it. Whether you're walking, driving, or taking public transportation, notice the sights, sounds, and sensations around you. Take full breaths and be completely present, changing a generally normal excursion into a chance for quiet.

3. Mindful Changes Between Tasks: While changing starting with one undertaking and then onto the next, stop briefly. Take a full breath and deliberately let go of the past undertaking. This helps clear the psyche and sets you up to move toward the following task with concentration and goal.

Integrating mindfulness into regular exercises changes them from unremarkable tasks into mindfulness practices that encourage mental clearness and quiet. It doesn't call for extra investment — simply a change in mindfulness.

Mindful breathing and development are amazing assets that assist professionals with remaining grounded and focused amid the requests of a bustling working day. Through practices like mindfulness breathing activities, gentle stretching, and walking meditation, you can develop a more emotional association with your body, discharge stress, and diminish stress. By integrating mindfulness into day-to-day exercises, every second turns into a chance for quiet and concentration, eventually upgrading your efficiency and prosperity.

Chapter 6: Mindful Communication and Relationships

Active listening and Mindful Communication

In the occupied and frequently high-stakes universe of work, discussions can undoubtedly become surged or zeroed in exclusively on prompt results. In any case, mindful communication — especially through active listening — empowers us to connect all the more genuinely with others. When polished reliably, it can lessen misconceptions, encourage trust, and lead to a more durable workplace.

Practicing Active listening

Active listening is at the center of mindful communication. It requires being completely present, hearing words as well as figuring out the purpose, emotions, and viewpoints behind them. By giving full consideration to a speaker, you convey regard and compassion, fabricating an establishment for more grounded proficient relationships.

To practice active listening:

1. Center Completely around the Speaker: Turn your body somewhat toward the speaker, visually engage, and put away any distractions like your telephone or PC. Exhibit your advantage with gestures or little certifications.

2. Tune in Without Judgment: Frequently, we tune in with a psychological channel, judging or deciphering words before the speaker wraps up. Mindful listening implies getting the message transparently, without untimely ends. This establishes a protected climate for the speaker to transparently put themselves out there.

3. Notice Nonverbal Prompts: Notice the speaker's non-verbal communication, looks, and tone. Some of the time, nonverbal prompts convey more significance than the actual words, giving a more emotional comprehension of their emotions and goals.

4. Stand by to Answer: Rather than setting up your answer while the other individual is talking, give yourself a second after they've completed the process of talking. Stopping extends regard and assists you with forming a more insightful and important reaction.

Reflecting and Paraphrasing

To exhibit that you genuinely comprehend what the other individual is talking about, work on reflecting and summarizing. This implies momentarily summing up their central issues and, if essential, posing explaining questions.

For instance, you could say, "It seems as though you're worried about complying with the time constraint given the ongoing responsibility. Is that right?" This procedure approves their sentiments, improves understanding, and helps clear up any misconceptions. Reflecting and summarizing can be important in proficient settings where exact communication is fundamental.

Building Mindful Relationships at Work

Work environment relationships assume an essential part in work fulfillment, efficiency, and in general prosperity. Mindful relationships are based on shared regard, sympathy, and open communication. By moving toward communications mindfully, you can cultivate a surer, cooperative workplace that benefits everybody.

Cultivating Compassion

Compassion is fundamental for building significant associations with partners. By imagining another's perspective, you can all the more likely comprehend their encounters and points of view, which thusly causes them to feel esteemed and upheld. Practicing sympathy doesn't need meaningful discussions — here and there, little motions are sufficient to convey understanding and empathy.

1. Show Appreciation: Basic affirmations, such as expressing gratitude toward a partner for their commitments, can go far in building compatibility and empowering future coordinated efforts.

2. Be Aware of Your Responses: During upsetting minutes, it's not difficult to hastily respond. Stopping before you answer somebody — particularly in testing discussions — exhibits persistence and regard. This mindful methodology evades miscommunications and keeps communications conscious.

3. Energize Inclusivity: Inclusivity implies inviting alternate points of view and permitting every individual's voice to be heard. While driving or partaking in group conversations, really try to incorporate calmer individuals. This training cultivates a more comprehensive and various work area.

Defining Solid Limits

Limits are fundamental for keeping up with conscious and useful relationships. Mindful limit setting permits you to attest your requirements while regarding others. In a professional setting, this could mean imparting your accessibility, overseeing assumptions for reaction times, or pleasantly declining demands when your responsibility is full.

Solid limits forestall burnout and make a common comprehension among partners. For instance, assuming you wind up wrecked with undertakings, it's proper to tell your group that you'll require additional opportunity to finish extra demands. Conveying limits early and mindfully can forestall errors and assist everybody with overseeing assumptions all the more successfully.

Managing Struggle with Mindfulness

Struggle in the work environment is unavoidable, however when drawn closer mindfully, it can turn into a chance for development and further developed communication. Mindful peacemaking includes moving toward conflicts with interest, receptiveness, and a pledge to settle issues usefully.

Perceiving Emotional Triggers

In clashes, emotions can heighten rapidly, blurring judgment and energizing errors. By becoming mindful of your emotional triggers, you can get receptive reactions early, permitting you to move toward the circumstance with a clearer brain.

At the point when you feel serious areas of strength for a reaction during a conflict, take a full breath and give yourself a second to deal with the inclination before answering. This short delay can have a tremendous effect on the way you handle the discussion, assisting you with staying away from rash responses.

Moving toward Discussions with Interest

Rather than accepting you know the other individual's expectations, move toward the discussion with interest. Pose unassuming questions, for example, "Could you at any point assist me with figuring out your viewpoint on this?" This procedure diffuses strain as well as exhibits regard for the other individual's perspective. Tuning in with a receptive outlook frequently uncovers basic issues or needs that, when tended to, can forestall comparable struggles from here on out.

Utilizing "I" Proclamations

While offering your viewpoints or sentiments in a contention, use "I" proclamations rather than "You" explanations. For instance, rather than saying, "You didn't uphold me on that task," say, "I felt unsupported on that venture, and I'd see the value in your criticism on how we can team up better."

"I" articulations center around your sentiments and encounters as opposed to finding fault, which can help the other individual answer all the more straightforwardly and forestall protective responses. This approach supports productive exchange and assists the two players with zeroing in on settling the issue as opposed to relegating shortcomings.

Mindful communication and relationships are key to establishing a positive workplace. By practicing active listening, building compassion, and overseeing struggle with a mindful methodology, you can cultivate more grounded, more useful associations with partners. These practices assist with decreasing errors, fabricate trust, and improve coordinated effort, prompting a better and really satisfying proficient life.

Part 3: Applying Mindfulness in the Workplace

Chapter 7: Mindfulness and Time Management

Prioritizing on Tasks with Mindfulness

The cutting edge working environment frequently requests quick independent direction, steady performing various tasks, and shuffling of numerous needs, all of which can prompt stress and burnout. Mindfulness offers an incredible asset for exploring these requests, assisting you with zeroing in on undertakings that really matter and dispense your time all the more successfully. By integrating mindfulness into using time productively, you can make more clear, more purposeful decisions about where to coordinate your energy.

The Power of Single-Tasking

Single-entrusting, or zeroing in on each undertaking in turn, is at the core of mindful using time productively. Studies have shown that performing various tasks really diminishes efficiency, increments blunders, and increases emotions of anxiety. Mindful using time effectively urges us to focus on one task, offer it our full consideration, and complete it prior to continuing on to the following.

To practice single-entrusting:
1. Begin with an Unmistakable Solution: Toward the start of every day or week, drill down undertakings in view of their significance and earnestness. Mindfully consider what genuinely requires your consideration and put forth reasonable boundaries.

2. Limit Distractions: Distinguish normal distractions (e.g., telephone notices, email alarms) and really try to limit them. For example, take a stab at quieting your telephone or utilizing program expansions to impede diverting sites while you work on basic undertakings.

3. Set Time Blocks for Centered Work: Apportion explicit periods over the course of the day committed to centered work. During these blocks, commit completely to a solitary task without changing to other people. After each block, enjoy some time off to reset prior to jumping into the following task.

4. Utilize Gentle Updates: It's not difficult to fall back into performing various tasks out of behavior pattern. Think about setting gentle updates (e.g., a tacky note directly in front of you) to remind yourself to remain present with each undertaking in turn. This little signal can assist with supporting the propensity for single-entrusting over the long haul.

By practicing single-entrusting, you can achieve undertakings all the more effectively, diminish stress, and develop a more prominent feeling of fulfillment in your work.

Applying the "Three Questions" Procedure

One method for focusing on undertakings mindfully is by utilizing a strategy called the "Three Questions" procedure. This approach urges you to stop and pose three questions before taking on another undertaking:

1. Is this task vital? Decide if the task is truly fundamental or on the other hand on the off chance that something can be deferred, appointed, or even eliminated.

2. Does this line up with my goals? Consider whether the undertaking lines up with your professional goals and values. On the off chance that it doesn't, it could merit rethinking its significance.

3. Will this add to my prosperity? Assess whether the task is probably going to upgrade or diminish your general prosperity. Mindful using time productively underscores undertakings that help efficiency as well as encourage a solid balance between serious and fun activities.

By posing these questions, you can guarantee that your emphasis stays on undertakings that seriously affect your work and individual prosperity.

Keeping away from Performing multiple tasks and Distractions

Performing multiple tasks can feel like a fundamental professionalism in quick-moving workplaces, yet research shows that it frequently prompts botches, diminished productivity, and more elevated levels of stress. By moving away from performing various tasks and overseeing distractions mindfully, you can turn out to be more useful and present in your work.

Perceiving the Expense of Performing various tasks

At the point when we perform various tasks, our minds quickly switch between undertakings as opposed to performing them all the while. This exchange comes at a mental expense, as each progress requires mental energy and prompts more slow execution generally. By understanding the limits of performing multiple tasks, we can embrace procedures that improve concentration and efficiency.

Practicing Mindfulness Advances

On the off chance that you want to switch undertakings over the day, mindfulness advances can assist with facilitating the shift and keeping up with the center. A mindfulness change includes stopping briefly between undertakings to reset and pull together. Requiring only a couple of moments to inhale emotionally, clear your psyche, and deliberately shift regard for the new task can decrease the psychological strain that frequently accompanies fast exchanging.

For instance:

1. End the Ongoing Undertaking with Purpose: Prior to continuing on toward another task, pause for a minute to finish off the past one. This could mean writing down notes or denoting the task as complete.

2. Take a Breathing Delay: Between undertakings, take a couple of slow, mindful breaths. This training assists your cerebrum with flagging the finish of one movement and sets it up to connect completely with the following.

3. Set a Goal for the New Undertaking: Consider what you desire to achieve with the new assignment. By setting a short goal, you make a feeling of direction and concentrate that can work on both efficiency and fulfillment.

Mindful Goal Setting

Goal setting is vital for compelling using time effectively, however goals can frequently feel overpowering on the off chance that they're not drawn closer mindfully. Mindful goal setting underscores higher standards when in doubt, assisting you with setting clear, sensible, and attainable goals that line up with your qualities.

Defining Clear and Practical Goals

Mindful goals are explicit, sensible, and lined up with your own and proficient goals. To put forth clear goals:

1. Be Explicit: Obscure goals, as "be more useful" or "finish work quicker," can feel overpowering and muddled. All things considered, separate bigger goals into explicit advances, for example, "complete one report by early afternoon" or "burn through 30 minutes on messages."

2. Set Quantifiable Achievements: Quantifiable goals give a feeling of progress. By setting benchmarks, you make more modest, feasible advances that amount to critical accomplishments over the long run. For example, on the off chance that you're dealing with an enormous undertaking, set achievements for each stage, like finishing research, drafting a diagram, or concluding a part.

3. Make an Equilibrium of Short and Long Haul Goals: A mindful methodology offsets quick necessities with future goals. Momentary goals can provide you with a feeling of everyday achievement, while long haul goals guarantee your work lines up with more extensive desires.

Practicing Self-Empathy in Goal Setting

Goal setting can now and then prompt stress, particularly assuming you feel forced to accomplish everything impeccably or rapidly. Practicing self-sympathy lessens this tension, permitting you to stay versatile in any event, when things don't go according to plan.

Recognize Your Cutoff Points: Comprehend that your energy and time are limited assets. Focus on goals that you can reasonably achieve inside your ongoing limit, and go ahead and your goals if necessary.

Observe Progress, Not Simply Consummation: Perceive and commend each move toward your goals, regardless of whether you haven't yet arrived at the end goal. Progress itself is a critical accomplishment, and recognizing it can keep you inspired and centered.

Gain from Difficulties: In the event that you experience mishaps, treat them as learning valuable open doors as opposed to disappointments. Considering mindful difficulties can assist you with changing your methodology and refining your goals for better progress from here on out.

Making a Mindful Plan for the Day

A mindful plan for the day goes past essentially posting undertakings; it stresses expectation, concentration, and solutions with your needs. Via cautiously organizing your rundown, you can keep your responsibility reasonable and lined up with your qualities.

1. Limit Your Everyday Tasks: Rather than filling your rundown with many undertakings, select a couple of fundamental things that line up with your goals. This forestalls overpower and permits you to focus completely on each undertaking.

2. Use Language That Reflects Goal: Rather than stating "Finish report," attempt "Devote centered opportunity to the report." This change in language supports a more purposeful, present-centered way to deal with each undertaking.

3. Ponder Each Undertaking's Motivation: For everything, momentarily think about its motivation and importance. Is it fundamental? Does it serve a bigger goal? Reflecting in this manner assists you with focusing on undertakings that are really significant and lined up with your goals.

Mindfulness changes using time effectively from an attempt to beat the odds into a purposeful, offset approach that lines up with your qualities. By focusing on single-entrusting, limiting distractions, putting forth mindful goals, and making a significant plan for the day, you can support both efficiency and fulfillment in your professional life. As you keep practicing mindful using time effectively, recall that consistency is vital. Little, mindful changes over the long haul can prompt huge enhancements in concentration, effectiveness, and in general prosperity.

Chapter 8: Mindfulness and Emotional Intelligence

Recognizing and Dealing with Emotions

The capacity to understand people on an emotional level (EQ) is a fundamental professionalism in the professional world, permitting us to explore complex social relationships, answer tranquility to unpleasant circumstances, and cultivate solid relationships. One of the fundamental parts of the capacity to appreciate anyone on a deeper level is the capacity to perceive and deal with emotions, both inside ourselves and in others. This mindfulness and guideline structure the reason for further developed independent direction, stress to the executives, and generally prosperity.

The Role of Mindfulness in Emotional Awareness

Mindfulness trains us to turn out to be more receptive to our viewpoints, sentiments, and actual sensations. By routinely practicing mindfulness, we develop an uplifted consciousness of our close-to-home reactions as they emerge, permitting us to notice them without quick judgment or response. For instance, during a bustling business day, you might experience disappointments or stressors that trigger disturbance, uneasiness, or even resentment. Through mindfulness, you can see these emotions right on time, before they heighten, and decide to answer as opposed to responding incautiously.

To develop emotional awareness through mindfulness:

1. Work on Seeing Your Emotions: Routinely check in with yourself during the day. Ask yourself, "What am I feeling at present?" and see without attempting to change it. Recognizing your emotions right off the bat keeps them from developing and prompting a responsive way of behaving.

2. Participate in Body Filtering: Emotions frequently manifest truly before we deliberately register them. By doing a speedy body examination — starting from the head to the toes — you can identify strain or distress that might demonstrate hidden emotions. This mindfulness can assist you with tending to these sentiments before they influence your temperament or associations.

3. Mark the Inclination: When you notice an inclination, name it with a particular name, for example, "stress," "dissatisfaction," or "stress." This basic demonstration of naming decreases the feeling's power and gives lucidity, making it more straightforward to valuably address the inclination.

Through these practices, mindfulness can extend your emotional mindfulness, permitting you to deal with your emotions more successfully as opposed to allowing them to control your activities.

Answering versus Reacting

One of the key differentiations that mindfulness cultivates is the distinction between responding and answering. Responding is a rash, programmed conduct driven by our emotions. Answering, then again, includes an insightful, estimated approach that thinks about the unique situation and the effect of our activities. In high-stress workplaces, having the option to answer rather than respond can be extraordinary.

Stop Before Acting: When confronted with a difficult circumstance, take a short delay. This could mean taking a couple of full breaths or building up to three preceding answers. This little respite makes supports between your underlying close-to-home response and your reaction.

Reevaluate Your Meditations: When you stop, attempt to reexamine what is happening positively or impartially. For instance, rather than thinking, "This is unreasonable," consider, "This is testing, yet I can deal with it." This reevaluation can assist with moving your outlook, permitting you to answer with quiet and clearness.

Center around Productive Communication: Mindfulness urges you to consider what your words and activities will mean for other people. By deliberately picking your reaction, you can convey it all the more productively, cultivating better getting it and cooperation with partners.

Creating Mindfulness and Self-Guideline

Mindfulness and self-guideline are at the center of the capacity to understand people on an emotional level. Mindfulness includes figuring out our inward motivations, assets, shortcomings, and close-to-home triggers, while self-guideline is the capacity to deal with these inner states. Mindfulness practices help develop both, enabling you to answer mindfully and handily in a scope of circumstances.

Building Mindfulness Through Meditation

Mindful meditation includes saving a couple of moments every day to survey your emotions, meditations, and ways of behaving. By routinely reflecting, you can foster a more emotional comprehension of your propensities and examples, as well as the elements that trigger explicit emotions.

Recognize Examples: Consider repeating emotions or circumstances that reliably trigger overwhelming inclinations. Seeing themes can help you expect and deal with these emotions all the more successfully.

Figure out Your Motivations: Invest energy investigating what drives you, particularly in the work environment. Ask yourself, "For what reason do I feel a sense of urgency to answer a specific way?" or "What am I expecting to accomplish in this present circumstance?" This self-assessment can carry lucidity to your activities, permitting you to adjust them to your qualities and goals.

Practice Non-Critical Mindfulness: During meditation, noticing your considerations and emotions without analysis or judgment is fundamental. This gentle methodology makes a place of refuge for self-investigation, decreasing preventiveness and empowering self-acknowledgment.

Improving Self-Guideline with Mindfulness Procedures

Mindfulness assists you with dealing with your emotions successfully by preparing your cerebrum to deal with stressors with versatility. Self-guideline becomes more straightforward when you're mindful of your emotions and have the devices to quiet and focus on yourself.

Breathing Strategies for Quiet: When you feel overpowered or baffled, utilize mindful breathing activities to quiet your sensory system. Slow, full breaths enact the body's unwinding reaction, assisting with diminishing stress and reestablishing the center.

Picture a Quiet Reaction: Before responding, pause for a minute to imagine a quiet and valuable reaction. Envisioning yourself taking mindfulness of the circumstance easily can assist with diminishing tension and lift certainty, making it more straightforward to answer nicely continuously.

Practice Everyday Meditation: Meditation prepares your brain to keep up with center and emotional equilibrium, in any event, during distressing circumstances. By reflecting consistently, you fortify your capacity to direct your emotions and remain grounded.

Mindful Navigation

Mindful navigation includes pursuing decisions with mindfulness and goal, considering both quick requirements and long-haul results. By moving toward choices mindfully, you can keep away from indiscreet decisions that might prompt lament and on second thought make results that line up with your qualities and goals.

Dialing Back the Dynamic Cycle

In speedy conditions, it's not difficult to feel compelled to rapidly decide. In any case, dialing back — even momentarily — can prompt more smart and successful decisions.

Interruption to Think about Choices: When confronted with a choice, respite to think about every conceivable choice. Indeed, even a short delay can give sufficient mental space to completely evaluate what is happening.

Weigh Transient versus Long Haul Effects: Mindfulness energizes a fair point of view that thinks about both quick advantages and expected long-haul results. Ask yourself, "What will this choice mean for me or my group from here on out?"

Ponder Solution with Values: Before pursuing a decision, consider whether it lines up with your guiding principle and professional goals. Mindfulness dynamic means to guarantee that your activities support your general reason, prompting more prominent fulfillment and less laments.

Practicing Acknowledgment of Unsure Results

Direction frequently includes a component of vulnerability. Practicing mindfulness can assist you with tolerating that a few results are outside of your reach, lessening nervousness, and advancing true serenity.

Discharge the Requirement for Conviction: Mindfulness trains us to relinquish unbending assumptions and embrace vulnerability as a characteristic piece of life. By delivering the requirement for a "great" result, you decrease the strain encompassing your choice.

Trust Your Instinct: Mindfulness cultivates self-trust, which is fundamental in navigation. At the point when decisions are muddled, depending on your instinct and previous encounters as guides, believing that you're fit for taking mindfulness of anything result emerges.

Acknowledge the Educational experience: Instead of dreading botches, view them as learning open doors. Each choice, whether fruitful or testing, gives significant experiences that can illuminate future decisions.

Developing Sympathy and Empathy

Sympathy and empathy are fundamental for building solid, positive relationships in the working environment. Mindfulness assists us with interfacing all the more emotionally with others by empowering us to listen mindfully, perceive their points of view, and answer with thoughtfulness.

Practicing Compassion Through Active listening

Active listening is a central part of mindful communication. At the point when we listen mindfully, we put away private inclinations, center completely around the speaker, and focus on them.

Tune in Without Interfering with: Permit others to articulate their thoughts completely prior to answering. This approach extends regard and encourages a stronger and more confiding in air.

Pose Explaining Questions: To show real interest, pose questions that urge the speaker to expand. This explains their viewpoint as well as exhibits your ability to emotionally grasp them.

Notice Non-Verbal Prompts: Focus on the speaker's non-verbal communication, tone, and looks. These prompts give a significant understanding of their emotions, assisting you with answering all the more humanely.

Answering with Empathy

Mindfulness cultivates empathy, empowering us to answer others with thoughtfulness and persistence, in any event, during clashes. Empathetic reactions can further develop group elements and establish a surer workplace.

Practice Viewpoint Taking: Attempt to see circumstances from others' perspectives. By taking into account their point of view, you're bound to answer with understanding and persistence.

Offer Steady Criticism: While giving input, outline your remarks in a way that is helpful and strong. Empathetic input advances development and reinforces relationships.

Develop Persistence: Mindfulness helps us to answer gradually and mindfully. Practicing persistence, particularly when emotions run high, can forestall errors and cultivate good associations.

Mindfulness and the capacity to understand people at their core remain closely connected, making a strong starting point for individual and professional achievement. By perceiving and dealing with emotions, practicing self-guidelines, and settling on mindful choices, you can explore working environment challenges with more prominent versatility and understanding. Furthermore, developing sympathy and empathy upgrades your relationships, advancing an amicable, steady climate. Through normal mindfulness practice, you fortify the capacity to understand people on a emotional level abilities that won't just further develop your work life yet additionally add to your general prosperity.

Chapter 9: Maintaining Motivation - Tips for Staying Focused and Disciplined

The Significance of Motivation and Discipline

Motivation and discipline are two vital elements for accomplishing individual and professional goals. While motivation gives the underlying push, discipline keeps us pushing ahead when excitement disappears. Many individuals start with fervor, just to battle with keeping up with force after some time. In any case, by understanding how to support motivation and building propensities that build up discipline, you can keep fixed on your goals, in any event, during testing times.

Motivation is much of the time affected by our close-to-home states, while discipline is established in the propensities and schedules we lay out. Both are fundamental for long-haul achievement, and each supports the other. Discipline keeps us advancing reliably, which thus fabricates motivation as we see improvement. Perceiving the interaction between these two powers can assist you with fostering a strong mentality, one that is ready to handle both momentary difficulties and long-haul goals.

Setting Clear, Reachable Goals

Quite possibly the earliest move toward keeping up with motivation is setting clear, practical goals. Explicit, quantifiable goals provide you with a feeling of guidance and a reasonable end highlight hold back nothing, and give a consistent wellspring of motivation. At the point when your goals are excessively ambiguous or excessively aggressive, feeling overpowered or lost is simple.

The Force of Present Moment and Long-Haul Goals

Setting both present moment and long haul goals gives a decent way to deal with making progress. Momentary goals assist with separating bigger desires into reasonable advances, offering a feeling of achievement end route. Long-haul goals, then again, keep you zeroed in on the master plan and give an enduring feeling of motivation.

Characterize Your Drawn-out Vision: Begin by distinguishing your definitive goal. What do you expect to accomplish in the following year, five years, or even 10 years? This vision goes about as your directing light, assisting you with remaining roused through difficulties and mishaps.

Break Goals into More Modest Achievements: Gap your drawn-out goal into more modest, significant stages. For instance, if your drawn-out goal is to finish a venture, set explicit month-to-month or week-after-week achievements. This gains ground feel achievable and keep motivation high as you arrive at every achievement.

Set "Stretch Goals" for Additional Motivation: notwithstanding reasonable goals, consider laying out stretch goals that challenge you to go a piece further. These optimistic targets push you out of your usual range of familiarity, providing you with a feeling of energy and empowering self-awareness.

Observing Little Wins

Perceiving and celebrating progress, regardless of how little, can support motivation. Every little accomplishment is a step in the right direction and an update that your endeavors are paying off. Festivities don't need to be intricate; even little rewards, such as enjoying some time off or indulging yourself with something pleasant, can build up your obligation to your goals.

Building a Standard that Supports Discipline

Discipline flourishes in organized conditions. At the point when you fabricate a daily schedule, you make a structure that makes it more straightforward to keep focused and kills the need to depend exclusively on motivation. A predictable routine lays out certain propensities, which after some time become natural, lessening the psychological exertion expected to remain trained.

The Job of Morning and Night Schedules

Laying out schedules toward the start and end of your day can make serious areas of strength for discipline. A morning schedule establishes a useful vibe for the afternoon, while a night schedule considers meditation and readiness.

Morning Schedule for Concentration and Energy: Begin your day with exercises that invigorate and concentrate your psyche. This could incorporate activity, mindfulness, or setting aims for the afternoon. An engaged beginning makes energy, making it more straightforward to remain restrained.

Evening Schedule for Meditation and Reset: Take the opportunity at night to survey the day, noticing any achievements or regions for development. This meditation supports discipline by keeping your goals on top of your psyche and permitting you to anticipate the following day.

Booking Time for High-Need Assignments

At the point when you plan explicit blocks of time for undertakings connected with your goals, you make a responsibility that builds up discipline. By assigning time for high-need exercises, you diminish the probability of tarrying and create a feeling of responsibility.

Use Time-Hindering: Commit blocks of time to explicit tasks or tasks. By assigning centered time for high-need undertakings, you limit distractions and increment efficiency.

Limit Choice Exhaustion: Make a standard that limits navigation, like arranging dinners, outfits, and your everyday schedule ahead of time. This permits you to moderate mental energy for significant undertakings and remain fixed on your goals.

Overcoming Procrastination and Staying Focused

Stalling is one of the greatest snags to keeping up with motivation and discipline. Perceiving the reason why we tarry and utilizing successful techniques to balance it can assist you with remaining on track and abstaining from falling behind.

Distinguishing Stalling Triggers

Understanding the reason why you tarry is the initial step to conquering it. Normal reasons incorporate apprehension about disappointment, hairsplitting, and feeling overpowered. By recognizing your particular triggers, you can address them all the more.

Break Undertakings into More Modest Advances: Huge assignments can feel overwhelming, prompting delay. By separating them into more modest advances, you make the interaction more reasonable and increase your motivation to get everything rolling.

Put down a Point in time Cutoff for Beginning: Focus on dealing with an undertaking for only five or ten minutes. Frequently, beginning is the hardest part. When you start, you're bound to proceed and follow through with the job.

Limiting Distractions

In this day and age, distractions are all over, making it trying to remain on track. By proactively dealing with your current circumstance, you can lessen distractions and keep up with your fixation.

Make a Committed Work area: Assign a particular region for work or goal-related tasks. Having a committed work area can further develop concentration and indicate to your mind that now is the ideal time to work.

Limit Computerized Distractions: Use instruments like site blockers or center applications to limit breaks from web-based entertainment or email. Assigning specific times for checking messages can assist you with remaining in a useful stream.

Developing a Development Outlook

A development outlook — the conviction that capacities and insight can be created through exertion and learning — is fundamental for supporting motivation and discipline. By embracing a development mentality, you view difficulties as any open doors for development as opposed to mishaps, which encourages versatility and industriousness.

Embracing Disappointment as a Learning A valuable open door

Individuals with a development outlook see disappointment as a characteristic piece of the educational experience. At the point when you experience snags, rather than feeling deterred, use them as any open doors to learn and get to the next level.

Consider Difficulties: When you face misfortunes, carve out an opportunity to think about what turned out badly and what you can gain from the experience. This meditation transforms disappointments into significant learning minutes.

Look for Productive Input: Criticism is an amazing asset for development. Productive analysis assists you with recognizing regions for development, permitting you to adjust and reinforce your methodology.

Practicing Self-Empathy

Motivation and discipline are challenging to support when you're excessively incredulous of yourself. Self-sympathy includes treating yourself with benevolence and understanding, particularly during troublesome times. At the point when you practice self-empathy, you're bound to remain strong and keep up with motivation.

Challenge Negative Self-Talk: Supplant self-decisive considerations with empowering ones. For instance, rather than saying, "I'll always be unable to do this," remind yourself, "This is a test, however, I can improve with exertion."

Reward Yourself for Exertion, Not Simply Results: Perceive the work you put in, no matter what the result. This builds up a development outlook and empowers diligence.

Building Responsibility

Responsibility is a strong motivation that can assist you with remaining trained. By imparting your goals to other people, you make a feeling of obligation to see everything through to completion.

Finding a Responsibility Accomplice

A responsible accomplice can offer help, consolation, and input. Pick somebody who has comparative goals or values and can keep you on target.

Normal Registrations: Schedule ordinary gatherings with your responsibility accomplice to talk about progress, difficulties, and plans. These registrations create a mood that supports discipline.

Observe Each Other's Victories: Perceive each other's accomplishments, regardless of how little. Gathering together to celebrate constructs motivation and fortifies the association.

Joining a Local area

Networks zeroed in on comparative goals, whether on the web or face to face, can offer extra help and motivation. By drawing in with other people who share your desires, you make an organization that encourages responsibility and discipline.

Take part in Gathering Difficulties: Gathering difficulties creates a common feeling of direction and urges you to remain focused.

Share Encounters and Counsel: Participating in discussions about difficulties, solutions, and progress with others can give you new bits of knowledge and propel you to continue to push ahead. Keeping up with motivation and discipline is a nonstop cycle that requires clear goals, compelling schedules, and a versatile outlook. By laying out reachable goals, laying out strong schedules, defeating hesitation, and developing a development mentality, you can foster the discipline expected to remain fixed on your way. Moreover, building responsibility through organizations and local area associations supports your obligation to your goals. With reliable exertion and a positive methodology, you can keep up with the motivation and discipline important to make long-haul progress.

Part 4: Maintaining Mindfulness

Chapter 10: Overcoming Mindfulness Obstacles

Mindfulness, really extraordinary, isn't without its difficulties. Occupied professionals, specifically, frequently face leaps that can make remaining steady with mindfulness practice troublesome. These hindrances, nonetheless, are not detours but instead valuable chances to fortify your obligation to mindfulness. By distinguishing normal difficulties and understanding how to address them, you can keep up with your motivation and coordinate mindfulness into your life, even in the most demanding circumstances. This part centers around down-to-earth methodologies to assist you with defeating normal snags and constructing a versatile mindfulness practice that perseveres.

Normal Difficulties and Solutions

Challenge 1: Time Imperatives

Quite possibly of the most incessant hindrances professionals face is setting aside opportunities for mindfulness. With plans loaded with gatherings, cutoff times, and individual obligations, cutting out even a couple of moments for a mindfulness practice can feel like an extravagance.

Solution: Begin Little and Assemble Slowly

Mindfulness doesn't need to require a huge time responsibility. Start with only five minutes every day, whether it's through a speedy breathing activity or a short mindful perception. Indeed, even a short delay can affect your psychological lucidity and concentration. After some time, as you experience the advantages, it becomes more straightforward to expand the term. You'll likewise possibly find that normal practice expands your effectiveness, making it simpler to make additional opportunities for mindfulness.

Challenge 2: Absence of Prompt Outcomes

Not at all like some efficiency hacks, the advantages of mindfulness aren't immediately evident 100% of the time. This can prompt disappointment and uncertainty about whether the training is advantageous.

Solution: Shift Concentration from Results to Experience

Mindfulness is tied in with being available with whatever emerges at the time, without judgment or assumption. The impacts might be unobtrusive from the start, and this requires a change in mentality. Instead of looking for speedy, substantial results, permit yourself to see the value in the experience of mindfulness itself. Notice little changes —, for example, a feeling of quiet after a concise meditation or an interruption before responding to an upsetting email. These steady advantages accumulate over the long haul, building flexibility and mindfulness.

Challenge 3: Physical and Mental Distress

It's not unexpected to feel truly fretful or intellectually occupied during mindfulness practice. Professionals frequently experience an inclination to browse messages, contemplate work, or even shift positions now and again while pondering.

Solution: Embrace the Distress

Distress is a characteristic piece of mindfulness practice. It can uncover areas of stress or stress in both your brain and body. Rather than opposing these sentiments, move toward them with interest. Ask yourself everything the distress is saying to you. Assuming you feel fretful, it could show that your psyche is excessively invigorated or that your body needs development. Recognize these sensations, take a couple of full breaths, and permit them to be essential for the experience. Over the long haul, this acknowledgment becomes more straightforward, and the actual uneasiness frequently decreases.

Keeping up with Motivation and Consistency

Keeping up with motivation for mindfulness practice requires both goal and consistency. Here are key methodologies to keep you locked in:

Set Clear Goals

At the point when motivation fades, an unmistakable goal can go about as an anchor. Recognize why you need to practice mindfulness. Could it be said that you are looking to diminish stress, further develop concentration, or feel more adjusted in your work-life dynamic? Record your aims and keep them apparent in your work area. Each time you see them, you'll be helped to remember the explanation for your work, making it more straightforward to remain inspired.

Coordinate Mindfulness with Existing Schedules

Consistency becomes more straightforward when mindfulness is incorporated into your day-to-day exercises. For instance, assuming you drive, utilize that time for mindful breathing or perception. On the off chance that you drink espresso every morning, take a couple of mindful tastes before plunging into work. Coordinating mindfulness into existing schedules diminishes the need to "add" something to your day — it turns out to be essential for what you as of now do.

Practice Self-Empathy

Consistency doesn't mean flawlessness. There might be days when mindfulness falls out of view. As opposed to being incredulous of yourself, practice self-empathy. Advise yourself that mindfulness is an excursion, not a goal, and each little exertion adds to your general advancement.

By permitting space for flaws, you fabricate a strong outlook that is bound to remain connected over the long haul.

Mindfulness in Testing Circumstances

Indeed, even with a reliable practice, mindfulness can be especially hard to keep up with in testing circumstances. Whether it's a high-stress meeting, an individual emergency, or an extraordinary responsibility, these minutes test your responsibility. Nonetheless, they likewise offer the best an open door for development.

Utilize Breathing as an Anchor

In snapshots of uplifted stress, your breath can act as a strong anchor. When confronted with a tough spot, take three full breaths, zeroing in on the vibe of the air entering and leaving your body. This straightforward strategy quiets your sensory system and makes a delay, permitting you to move toward the circumstance with more noteworthy clearness.

Rethink Distressing Circumstances

Mindfulness instructs us that our view of an occasion frequently impacts our reaction more than the actual occasion. When stood up to a difficult circumstance, have a go at reexamining it. Rather than review it as an obstruction, think of it as an amazing chance to practice flexibility and persistence. This change in context diminishes close-to-home reactivity, assisting you with staying engaged and quiet.

Make Mindful Breaks During the Day

In high-stress conditions, brief mindfulness breaks can be important. Regardless of whether it's only 30 seconds, stop, inhale, and reconnect with the current second. This training doesn't interfere with your work process however upgrades it by permitting you to reset. After some time, these brief breaks develop a more noteworthy feeling of equilibrium and forestall burnout.

Building a Strong Mindfulness Practice

To support a mindfulness practice over the long haul, incorporating versatility into your approach is significant. Life's requests will vary, and your training ought to be sufficiently adaptable to adjust.

Foster an Emotionally supportive network.

Share your mindfulness process with associates, companions, or relatives. Having an emotionally supportive network can build up your responsibility and give consolation during troublesome periods. A few working environments considerably offer mindfulness gatherings or studios, which can be an incredible method for remaining drawn in with similar people.

Consider Your Advancement Routinely

At regular intervals, pause for a minute to consider your mindfulness practice. Consider any sure changes you've seen, like superior concentration, diminished stress, or a more prominent feeling of quiet. Recognizing your advancement supports motivation and assists you with remaining predictable. It likewise permits you to change your training in light of what's functioning admirably and what might require refinement.

Be Available to Changing Your Training

Mindfulness is certainly not a one-size-fits-all solution. As you progress, you might find that specific methods work better compared to other people, or that your requirements develop over the long haul. Be available to change your training to suit these changes. Explore different avenues regarding new methods, investigate different meditation styles, or take a stab at different lengths of your meetings. Adaptability keeps your training pertinent and lined up with your self-awareness.

Chapter 11: Mindfulness and Self-Mindfulness

In a speedy existence where requests for our significant investment appear to be consistent, the idea of taking mindfulness of oneself can frequently feel like an extravagance as opposed to a need. However, focusing on taking mindfulness of oneself and developing mindfulness are fundamental practices that anchor us amid life's difficulties. This section digs into the significance of focusing on taking mindfulness of oneself, practicing mindful self-empathy, and building flexibility — all vital components in making a reasonable, satisfied life.

Focusing on Taking mindfulness of oneself

At its center, taking mindfulness of oneself is tied in with perceiving your requirements and regarding your prosperity. It's not self-centered to require investment for yourself; rather, a fundamental practice engages you to appear as the best version of yourself in each everyday issue. Focusing on mindfulness of oneself means embracing a mentality that values rest, meditation, and exercises that support both brain and body.

Taking mindfulness of oneself is certainly not a one-size-fits-all methodology but instead an emotionally private practice. While some might discover a sense of harmony in calm meditation, others might re-energize through actual work, social associations, or imaginative pursuits. The key is to recognize the practices that resound most with you and coordinate them into your daily schedule with aim.

Moves toward Focus on Taking mindfulness of oneself

1. Set Boundaries

Defining limits is a central part of being mindful of oneself. By obviously characterizing what you endlessly won't endure in that frame of mind of your life — be it work, relationships, or individual time — you make a defensive space for your energy and mental prosperity. Limits permit you to deal with your time all the more actually and lessen sensations of overpowering, guaranteeing that you can routinely take part in mindfulness of yourself.

2. Plan Taking mindfulness of oneself

Taking mindfulness of oneself as a fundamental solution in your schedule supports its significance. Shut out devoted time every week, and regard it as you would some other responsibility. Whether it's a day-to-day meditation meeting, a night walk, or time to seek after a side interest, consistency is key in building a mindfulness of oneself propensity that upholds long-haul prosperity.

3. Pay listening to Your Body

Frequently, our bodies signal when we want to rest, develop, or sustenance, however, in the surge of day-to-day existence, these prompts can be barely noticeable. Practicing mindfulness assists us with tuning into these inconspicuous signs, permitting us to answer with the fitting type of mindfulness. Focusing on your body's necessities is one of the best ways of remaining grounded and stimulated.

4. Work on Saying No

Saying "no" can be engaging, particularly when it safeguards your significant investment for taking mindful of oneself. At the point when solicitations emerge that don't line up with your needs or values, consider whether satisfying them is important. By specifically picking where to concentrate your energy, you can all the more likely oversee stress and make space for taking mindfulness of oneself exercises.

Mindful Self-Sympathy

Mindful self-sympathy includes treating yourself with the very benevolence and understanding that you would propose to a companion. It is a training established in recognizing your own humankind, flaws, and the difficulties you experience. By practicing self-sympathy, you develop versatility, decrease self-analysis, and encourage a more certain relationship with yourself.

Embracing Self-Sympathy

Mindfulness self-sympathy is about more than being gentle with yourself; it's tied in with recognizing you are enduring without judgment and offering to figure out its place. The three center components of self-empathy are:

1. Self-Graciousness

Self-graciousness implies addressing yourself with warmth, support, and grasping, in any event, during troublesome minutes. Rather than censuring yourself for slip-ups or deficiencies, work on insisting on your endeavors and recognizing your advancement. Self-thoughtfulness lessens nervousness and stress, establishing a strong mental climate for development.

2. Normal Humankind

Normal humankind is the comprehension that everybody faces difficulties, misfortunes, and deep-seated insecurities on occasion. At the point when we perceive that enduring is important for the common human experience, it becomes simpler to be gentle with ourselves. Embracing normal mankind lightens sensations of segregation and advises us that battles don't characterize us.

3. Mindful Awareness

Mindfulness urges us to notice our emotions and considerations without becoming connected to them. Practicing mindfulness permits us to recognize troublesome sentiments — whether bitterness, dissatisfaction, or disillusionment — without judgment. By remaining present in our encounters, we encourage more noteworthy acknowledgment and sympathy toward ourselves.

Commonsense Self-Sympathy Activities

1. Cherishing Generosity Meditation

Cherishing generosity meditation includes coordinating empathetic considerations toward yourself as well as other people. Begin by sitting discreetly, shutting your eyes, and rehashing phrases like, "May I be protected, may I be cheerful, may I be calm." Progressively, stretch out these desires to other people, including friends and family and, surprisingly, those you might view as trying. This training sustains compassion and advances a feeling of internal harmony.

2. The Self-Sympathy Break

During snapshots of stress, a fast self-sympathy break can significantly ground. Take a full breath, recognize the trouble of the circumstance, and remind yourself, "This is a snapshot of misery, enduring is a piece of life, may I be thoughtful to myself." This basic activity assists you with answering stress with mindfulness as opposed to self-analysis.

3. Composing a Self-Sympathetic Letter

Composing a letter to yourself is a strong method for practicing self-sympathy. Envision that you're keeping in touch with a going through an extreme companion time, and stretch out a similar comprehension to yourself. This exercise can move your point of view, offering solace and consolation amid trouble.

Building Strength

Strength is the capacity to explore difficulty, adjust to change, and return from mishaps. While taking mindfulness of oneself and self-empathy assist with building versatility by giving a groundwork of solidarity, flexibility itself is a professionalism that can be developed through mindful practices and purposeful ways of behaving. Building flexibility improves psychological wellness as well as supports long-haul prosperity by preparing you to deal with life's unavoidable high points and low points with elegance.

Techniques for Developing Strength

1. Embrace a Development Mentality

A development outlook includes seeing difficulties as any open doors for self-awareness. Rather than feeling crushed by mishaps, work on reexamining them as growth opportunities. This point of view diminishes sensations of disappointment and advances flexibility by empowering versatility and receptiveness.

2. Put forth Sensible Goals

Laying out attainable, significant goals gives guidance and motivation. Begin with little, reasonable goals that line up with your qualities, and commend every achievement en route. By defining and pursuing goals, you foster a feeling of direction and construct trust in your capacity to conquer obstructions.

3. Practice Appreciation

Appreciation is a useful asset for flexibility, as it shifts center based on what's turning out badly to what's working out positively. Have a go at keeping an appreciation diary, where you list three things you're thankful for every day. Over the long run, this propensity can change your outlook, cultivating motivation and versatility.

4. Look for Social Help

Associating with steady companions, family, or local area individuals can give close-to-home strength and viewpoint during troublesome times. Go ahead and out for help when required; flexibility isn't tied in with acting like a lone ranger yet about perceiving when to rest on others.

5. Participate in Customary Mindfulness Practice

Practicing mindfulness fortifies versatility by assisting you with remaining present, overseeing stress, and diminishing close-to-home reactivity. Customary mindfulness practice, whether through meditation, yoga, or mindful breathing, empowers you to move toward difficulties with more prominent clearness and quiet.

Coordinating Taking mindfulness of oneself, Self-Sympathy, and Flexibility

Taking mindfulness of oneself, self-empathy, and strength are associated practices. Everyone supports the other, making a groundwork of mental and emotional strength. By focusing on taking mindfulness of oneself, you develop an outlook that esteems your prosperity; through self-sympathy, you fabricate the compassion expected to explore life's difficulties; and by creating versatility, you engage yourself to beat difficulty with persistence and assurance.

When incorporated into day-to-day existence, these practices make an all-encompassing way to deal with health. They permit you to answer stress usefully, embrace defects with thoughtfulness, and face mishaps with fortitude. Each mindful decision you make to focus on yourself — whether through mindfulness of your schedules, empathetic self-talk, or flexibility-building exercises — adds to a decent, satisfying life.

Conclusion

In the present high-speed proficient scene, mindfulness offers help to more noteworthy concentration, versatility, and prosperity. All through this book, we have investigated an assortment of mindfulness practices custom-fitted for occupied professionals — each intended to ease stress, upgrade efficiency, and further develop work environment relationships. By figuring out the study of mindfulness, consolidating useful methods, and applying them straightforwardly inside the work environment, you currently have the devices to make a more adjusted and satisfying vocation.

Key important points underscore that mindfulness is in excess of a professionalism; a way of life that enables you to move toward every day with expectation, quiet, and clarity. From mindful breathing to building the ability to understand people at their core and self-sympathy, these procedures offer basic yet strong ways of remaining grounded amid requests.

Presently, now is the ideal time to make a move. Start incorporating these mindfulness practices step by step, perceiving that the actual excursion is all around as important as the goal. As you focus on your psychological prosperity, you'll end up better outfitted to lead with compassion, oversee stress, and accomplish an amicable balance between serious and fun activities. Here's to a mindful way ahead, where quiet and efficiency remain closely connected.